GW00660712

RECIPES TO
RELISH

The **Hallamshire** Press 1998

© 1998 The Hallamshire Press

Published by The Hallamshire Press
The Hallamshire Press is an imprint of
Interleaf Productions Limited
Broom Hall
Sheffield S10 2DR
England

Designed and typeset by
Interleaf Productions Limited
Printed in Singapore

British Library Cataloguing in Publication Data:
   A catalogue record for this book is available from the British Library

   ISBN 1874718 23 7

Contents

Donation

For every copy of this book sold – 50p will be donated to The Children's Appeal

The Sheffield Children's Hospital was established on its current site in 1876 where the building now forms the administrative area of the hospital. It is one of only eight dedicated children's hospitals in the country providing specialist care from birth to 16 years of age. The primary catchment area is the North Trent region but patients are referred from all over the country. The hospital is intensely proud of its pioneering work into the causes of childhood illnesses, their prevention and cure.

Care is provided in ten wards, from intensive care to day care, through medical and surgical specialities, including neo-natal surgery, oncology, ENT, plastic surgery, orthopaedics and general. There are currently four operating theatres performing more than twenty operations each day and an Accident and Emergency Department that is open 24 hours a day, 365 days a year.

The Children's has undergone many building changes over the years which still continue today with the building work on the long-awaited new block at the rear of the hospital (Phase II) which started in April 1998.

A unique combination of facilities, expertise and understanding is offered by the hospital and it enjoys great support in Sheffield from local people, industry and retail. The vital funds raised by the Sheffield Children's Hospital Appeal are channelled into essential medical research and major new initiatives enabling us to lead as a national centre of excellence.

Our current priorities include a much needed purpose-designed cystic fibrosis centre and also the very latest technology to screen new born babies for inherited disorders which, if detected early, can be treated immediately—so avoiding serious illness. The Appeal also contributes to the continual improvement of the amenities that make our hospital homely for children and their families.

On behalf of the young patients who benefit from the exceptional services of The Sheffield Children's Hospital we offer our sincere thanks for your support.

Sheffield Children's Hospital

Registered charity number 505002

Foreword

I am pleased to have been asked to contribute a foreword for the Henderson's Relish Recipe Book. This book features some of Sheffield's best, not least of which is Henderson's Relish itself, a much-loved local delicacy whose reputation is spreading beyond the city's boundaries. *Recipes to Relish* contains recipes from some of our top restaurants and anecdotes from Sheffield celebrities.

Sheffield has always been recognised as the Steel City, but today it has much more to offer and to be proud of. The city is now a leader in sport and culture, shopping, travel, education, leisure and entertainment and has a wide choice of restaurants and eating places.

I am particularly delighted that a donation from the sale of each book will be made to the *Children's Appeal* at the Sheffield Children's Hospital.

I hope you enjoy reading the book and experimenting with some of the tasty recipes.

Frank White
Lord Mayor of Sheffield
September 1998

Publisher's Foreword

I was born in Sheffield and, except for a short time, I have always lived here. My mother was a good cook and always managed to produce good wholesome meals on a very small budget. Amazingly, no matter how many people turned up unexpectedly at meal times, she always managed to provide us all with a good helping of whatever was on offer that day. Most winter evenings when I came home from school there was a cup of hot gravy to be had in the kitchen, just waiting for the addition of few drops of Henderson's Relish, before I could sit down by the fire to enjoy it.

Henderson's was always there. From being very young I had to have lashings on Ash[1] and Meat & Potato Pie, both of which are still at the top of my list of favourite meals. Every Fish and Chip Shop had Henderson's on the counter and then of course there were the Pie & Pea Shops. Often these were just someone's front room with a counter and an oven. The one we used to frequent was at the bottom of Woodseats Road. The aroma was wonderful – really mouth-watering. Her meat pies were oval and it used to fascinate me as a child how skilful she was at wrapping them. There was a neat pile of greaseproof paper on the counter in the middle of which she stood the pie, the gravy was poured on and then, on the top – which was indented, were piled the mushy peas, finally a liberal spinkling of Henderson's Relish. The lady would then, with practised ease, fold this into a very neat parcel and then wrap the whole thing again in newspaper. Always the pie stayed upright and not a drop was spilt.

Of course I still use Henderson's, not only as a garnish on my old favourites but as an ingredient in cooking and marinades. Before barbecuing try: equal parts virgin olive oil and Henderson's, the juice of half a lemon, lots of black & red pepper and a pinch of salt – wonderful as a marinade for chicken.

I have included some of my own old favourties and some new vegetarian recipes for you to try (pages 75–80). I do hope you enjoy them and the rest of the super recipes included in this book. Don't forget be daring and use plenty of HENDERSON'S.

---

1. The origin of Ash is unclear. Many presume that it is Hash without the H, others however, believe that it is connected with Ash Wednesday and the beginning of Lent.

Pauline Climpson
Publisher, The Hallamshire Press
September 1998

Introduction

At Henderson's we decided that we wanted to raise the awareness of using Relish as a cooking ingredient rather than a garnish. With the current vogue for buying cooking ingredients, as opposed to ready meals, we were conscious of the fact that people in Sheffield had been using other types of sauces in their cooking, unaware of the culinary greatness of Sheffield's finest relish. Also, unlike most other sauces of its kind, Henderson's is suitable for vegetarians and this was something that we wanted to make people aware of.

I met up with Mike Morphew, Divisional Manager of Hospitality and Catering at The Sheffield College, and former Chef to Her Majesty the Queen. Together with John Janiszewski, Section Leader of Hospitality and Catering, we set about thinking of how to run a competition for students using Henderson's Relish as a cooking ingredient. Both Mike and John believed that some of the City's top chefs already used Relish in their cooking and so, with this in mind, we decided to take the competition out to the Chefs of Sheffield. It was encouraging for me to find out how highly the chefs rated Henderson's Relish.

After months of preparation we finally held the competition in the kitchens of The Sheffield College. We held two 50-minute Cook-Offs to find the winner. Several crates of Henderson's later, Wayne Bosworth, of Michelin rated Rafters Restaurant, was declared the winner. Wayne walked away with the trophy plus two tickets to be the personal guest of Peter Stringfellow at his club, and an invitation to join TV chef, Brian Turner, at his exclusive restaurant in Chelsea.

We then compiled a list of Sheffield celebrities, some exiled and some still living in Sheffield, who were 'Relish Rooters'. All those we approached were more than happy to devote some time to writing their own anecdote about Henderson's and I would like to thank them here for their time and effort. Together with our friends at The Hallamshire Press we then set about piecing together a book that would interest the people of Sheffield and, who knows how far, beyond.

Special thanks go to Mike Morphew, Gerry Webster, Brian Turner, Bobby Knutt, and Andrew Fyfe of The Hallamshire Press, their help, time and experience proved invaluable.

Remember! Next time you cook or eat a meal, don't just enjoy it—make sure you RELISH it!

Simon Webster
Henderson's, Sheffield
September, 1998

The Winner of Henderson's Recipes to Relish Competition

Wayne Bosworth of Rafters Restaurant

The Contestants

The winner,
Wayne Bosworth,
being presented with
the trophy by
Simon Webster,
with Dr Freeman,
MD of Henderson's,
and Mike Morphew

Fetching the Beer

George Cunningham was famous for his paintings of Sheffield in the 1930s. This one from his book *By George* depicts the inside of a typical Beer-On of the day, a wide variety of goods is displayed on the shelves – including, of course, Henderson's.

The Story So Far

It was Henry Henderson who began manufacturing the famous Henderson's Relish back in the latter part of the last century. Originally manufactured in Broad Lane, Sheffield, the product's appeal was immediate and the Company soon moved to better premises at Leavygreave Road. In 1940 the Company became Limited and Charles Hinksman was Chairman and Managing Director.

By the early Sixties Henderson's had moved again, further down the road to the Company's current premises at 41 Leavygreave Road. Throughout these upheavals Henderson's have never strayed further than half a mile from where Henry Henderson filled his first bottle of Relish.

The control of the Company has been in the hands of the Freeman family since the death of Charles Hinksman, with his wife, Gladys Hinksman, (née Freeman) taking control. By 1991, Dr Kenneth Freeman, nephew of the late Charles Hinksman, had become Managing Director and it is he who remains in charge to this day.

Henderson's is a household name in the City of Sheffield with many of its inhabitants Relish fans almost from birth. We are now supplying stores further afield, stretching to all corners of Yorkshire, as well as crossing the County borders into Derbyshire, Lancashire and Nottinghamshire.

We send our famous Relish out to ex-Sheffielders all over England and indeed, the world. No matter which part of the world they are in they find that there is nothing quite like the taste of Henderson's Relish.

Henderson's
Garlic & Horseradish Salsa
for Steak

Ingredients

1 clove crushed garlic
2 tablespoons grated horseradish
10oz (300g) chopped spring onion & tarragon
$1/3$ pint (200ml) olive oil
3 tablespoons Henderson's Relish

Method

Whisk together all the ingredients, season with salt
and pepper and serve with grilled steak.

Henderson's Coarse Grain Mustard & Herb Marinade

Ingredients

2 tablespoons coarse grain mustard
$1/3$ pint (200ml) olive oil
1 pinch coarse cracked black pepper
2 chopped shallots
5 tablespoons Henderson's Relish

Method

Mix all the ingredients together for the marinade, then marinate your chosen meat overnight.
Grill, shallow-fry or barbecue your meat.

Salad Salsa Verde with Henderson's Caramel

Ingredients

1 sprig chopped tarragon
1 sprig chopped basil
1 sprig chopped mint
1 sprig chopped coriander
1 sprig chopped chives
1 oz (25g) chopped spring onion
1 oz (25g) grated Parmesan
1 clove of crushed garlic
$^1/_2$ pint (300ml) olive oil
$^1/_3$ pint (200ml) Henderson's Relish

Method

Place all herbs, grated Parmesan, olive oil and garlic in a food processor and liquidise to a paste.

Reduce Henderson's Relish on the stove by two-thirds to a caramel. Add the Henderson's to the herb purée and stir in well.

This dressing can be used as a sauce for fish, salads and many other things as it is a very versatile dressing with lots of flavour.

Henderson's Velvet

Ingredients

Sugar lumps
Henderson's Relish
1 bottle of good quality sparkling wine
2 bottles or cans of your favourite stout

Method

Put some sugar lumps on a plate or saucer and soak them in Henderson's Relish.

Put one in each glass—use tall glasses as they help to keep the bubbles in.

Half-fill each glass with sparkling wine, then top them up with stout—be careful not to pour too quickly otherwise you will end up with a glass of froth and no wine.

Warning

If you drink more than two, you are likely to have an irresistible urge to say 'Good 'ealth luv' to the nearest person—so ensure that you are drinking with friends!

Good 'ealth luv!

All Henderson's recipes by Wayne Bosworth, of Michelin Rated Rafters Restaurant.

RELISHERS

Brendan Ingle

Throughout my years in Sheffield I have always loved the old blackstuff. In stews and casseroles, but especially on my Meat and Potato Pie, I pour on plenty of Relish.

I've trained many World Champions on the stuff. In my gym I have got Ryan Rhodes, Johnny Nelson, John Thaxdon and Pele Reid, all right up at the top of their respective championships, and all have benefited from a splash of the Henderson's. In fact Ryan informs me that even he thinks that Henderson's is unbeatable.

When the lads have a bite to eat down at the gym we pass round the Relish and it's proved to be a real knockout with them. We all certainly agree that Henderson's is the World Champion of Relishes. So, if any of you youngsters out there think you could make it as a Champion, start off with Relish—give your food the left-right combination when splashing it all over with Henderson's.

Sean Bean

I once bought two gallons of Henderson's Relish because I'd heard a rumour that they were packing up the business. This turned out to be untrue, however, I had enough Relish to last me for quite some time.

It's best, I think, on northern fish and chips, and I particularly enjoy mopping it up off the plate when I've finished with a rolled-up piece of buttered, white, sliced bread.

A fine brew.

Peter Stringfellow

My own special memories of Henderson's Relish are from when I was around nine or ten years old. We never had ketchup in our house, it was always Relish—morning, noon or night. I always remember my old mum's Ash which we covered with Relish, you couldn't have Ash without Henderson's. My mum made the best gravy in town, laced with Relish. I still picture her by the big cooker, a proper Yorkshire stove, I can still taste the Rabbit Stew and Dumplings she made and the Rabbit Pie all liberally lashed with our favourite brew.

When I first came down to London, the girls had never heard of Relish never mind Henderson's so my first breakfasts down here were missing that most vital of ingredients. It wasn't long before I was bringing it back in bulk from Sheffield to stock up my cupboards and, to this day, I always have Henderson's Relish on my bacon and eggs when I get up from the night before.

Families in Sheffield always had Relish, everyone used it, in everything. It became part of my childhood, my earliest memories and certainly the best ones. I've grown up with Henderson's and it will always be a little piece of Sheffield, not just in my pantry but also in my heart.

Rick Savage, Def Leppard

No matter where in the world we travel, we always make sure that we've got a bottle of Henderson's with us. Over the years we've driven our tour manager, Malvin, completely mad, refusing to eat any of the pies that he feeds us, without Henderson's Relish.

Every time that we come back to Sheffield we always make sure that we stock up with plenty of bottles. For the opening of our Players Bar Café we made sure that all our friends and guests were served up helpings of Meat and Potato Pie topped with the best Relish in the world.

When we've played in South America or India, the rest of the crew have tried to make sure that we have plenty of bottled water, but our main priority has always been bottles of Relish and making sure that they are packed.

Henderson's has rocked all over the world with us, whether it be Melbourne, Milan, Massachusetts or Manchester, you can always be sure the lads will be asking to 'Pour some Relish on me'.

Joe Scarborough

A Confession

Well doctor, it all began at school. My first act of defiance was to bunk off school at dinnertime, it was both secretive and dangerous—you could get a clip round the ear 'ole if you were late back. I spent my dinner money in a pie shop on Middlewood Road. It was here that I first came across the black bottle with the orange label.

This led to visits to the wilder side of town, in fact to Butler's Eating House where the dark liquor was freely available—it was heaven! I have since done three paintings of this place and a tearful Mr Butler has begged me to do no more!

Private pleasure has led me to public pride. Once, being invited to the annual Cutlers' Feast, I ordered a bottle of the beloved sauce for my main course. The stunned silence of my fellow table guests was only matched by the admiring glances from the ladies of Fretwell Downing.

Well as confession is good for the soul, here goes. My name is Joe Scarborough, and I am a Henderson's Relish addict! There now, that's better.

You don't fancy a crispy bacon sandwich, with a few drops of...?

Joe Ashton
MP *for Bassetlaw*

It is fifty-odd years since my granddad introduced me to Henderson's Relish. In those days it had hard red sealing-wax over the cork 'to keep the "bookay" in', my granddad said. Using a cobbler's awl, he would carefully break the seal and pierce a hole through the cork so that he could sprinkle the Relish.

That Relish had a secret recipe, he said. From the mysterious Orient. He claimed that soldiers in the Yorks and Lancs in the First World War would drink pints of it to get out of the trenches. They reckoned that when it came to blood tests, those poncey army doctors down south couldn't recognise it and would think the lads had contracted some mysterious ailment which qualified them for instant demob—he was a bit of a romancer, my granddad.

Whatever it was, it's been a narcotic fix for me ever since. No pork pie, ham shank, stew, sausage, mushy peas, kidney gravy or stuffing, can ever reach perfection without Henderson's Relish. I have wined and dined in Embassies from Washington to Tokyo without ever once tasting a sauce anywhere near its special flavour.

All basic peasant foods in every country have their own mixes. From curry to pepper to chilli, soy sauce to mozzarella cheese, and even jam in Poland. Often concocted years before fridges were invented simply to disguise the smell when the meat went off.

In the Houses of Parliament, new Labour cooks dress up yesterday's left-overs and announce them on the menu as pickled samphire, mascarpone, cardamom, sabayon and even tabbouleh (please don't ask me what these are), but never Henderson's Relish.

It's a waste of time asking for it. Unfortunately nobody outside the Sheffield area has ever heard of it. A1 steak sauce in the American supermarkets is not bad, but has nowhere near the fine delicate flavour and aroma of Henderson's.

Sadly these days, like all other blokes who have lived too well, I get gout. All alcohol, spicy foods and acids have to be carefully watched and weighed up as to whether the taste and satisfaction is worth the pain. Ounce for ounce, Henderson's Relish is worth every wince.

Tony Capstick

I had never heard of Henderson's Relish as a boy in Mexborough. Oh, we had sauces and condiments alright. Doctor Culpepper's Rhubarb Paste, Arkwright's Sausage Enhancer and Blind Jack o'Knaresborough's Chilli and Brimstone Vinegar (also useful for black-leading Yorkshire ranges).

Later, when I came to frequent the flesh pots of Sheffield, I would hear the name Henderson's Relish being whispered in the darker corners of various unsavoury kips and I started to recognise the signs of addiction to this most secret concoction.

The strange laughter, the feverish bright eyes, the saliva drooling down the chin. My mam made me promise that I would never try it. Then I met the Sheffield temptress with whom I am living over the brush at present.

Like all the other dee-dahs she was unable to eat anything unless it was lavishly drenched in this devilish brew. Once, just once, I ate a Meat and Tater Pie with Henderson's Relish—that was it. Today the temptress and I get through eleven bottles a week. Sorry Mam!

Tony Capstick can be found chatting away whilst dragging camera crews along on his walks which he undertakes for the BBC. Otherwise he can be heard each weekday hosting his own show on BBC Radio Dee-Dah (Sheffield). Having partially retired from his previous job as a 'recording artist', we are now hopeful that Tony will join together with his great mate Knutty in helping Henderson's Relish conquer the world.

Bobby Knutt

Bobby Knutt first started out working on the club scene throughout the North of England. Throughout this successful period he could always be seen playing a variety of characters in the annual pantomimes in the area.

Bobby now splits his time between playing loveable rogue, Albert Dingle, on YTV's Emmerdale; starring as the voice for the Tetley Tea adverts on TV; and performing his comedy act on cruises throughout the world. A much loved local celebrity, Bobby still lives in Sheffield and has decided to devote the rest of his life to mocking ferrets and helping Henderson's Relish conquer the World.

Knutty's Recipes

Knutty Lamb

Simply take some lamb chump chops or Barnsley chops. Place them in a dish and pour over Henderson's Relish until they are completely covered. Then sprinkle liberally with dried mixed herbs. Leave the chops marinating for 24 hours, turning occasionally. Take the chops out of the marinade and place on a grilling tray. Grill them on a moderate heat until they are done. These will taste delicious—they are also ideal for a barbecue and the aroma is absolutely superb.

Shiregreen Mock Ferret on Toast

First of all take one fresh ferret. To determine the freshness of the ferret, stick a pin in it—if it bites your thumb off, the ferret is fresh. You will note the title of this delicacy is Shiregreen Mock Ferret on Toast, so you must obtain a Shiregreen Mocking Barrel (a bucket will not do as the zinc impairs the flavour of the ferret). These mocking barrels are rare, and much sought after by gourmets the world over, but can still, occasionally, be purchased from Hiram and Minnie Mousetrouser Limited of Hatfield House Lane.

The barrel is about three feet deep and, once the ferret is in the barrel, an effective escape is virtually impossible. Place the ferret in it and begin to mock it by saying things like 'Oh what a silly ferret you are'. This will demoralise the once-proud ferret who should now willingly co-operate.

Next, place the ferret on the toast, you may find at this point that the ferret will keep walking away. Should this occur, affix the ferret to the toast with some Ellison Ferret Toast Staples—these can be purchased at any branch of the Albanian Bugatti Owners Club. Simmer the ferret (in its jacket) in the River Don for three days. If the ferret does not have a jacket you may use your own. Splash liberally with Henderson's Relish and serve immediately.

POSH NOSH

The
Abbeydale Restaurant

University House, Western Bank, Sheffield
Telephone 0114 222 8999

Modern British cooking, executed with great flair and served in a relaxed and efficient manner, is available right on your doorstep.

Executive Chef, Tracy Carr, and the staff invite you to join the growing band of loyal diners attracted by the seasonal lunch-time menus. With a recent review by Martin Dawes of the *Sheffield Star* rating the Abbeydale Restaurant's food five out of five for both quality and value, now is definitely the time to see for yourself.

The Abbeydale Restaurant is situated on level five of University House. To book or for further details telephone Marion Green.

Open Monday–Friday 12.00–2.00 p.m.

Loin of Rabbit
in White Onion Gravy

by
Tracy Carr
Executive Chef at The Abbeydale Restaurant

Loin of Rabbit in White Onion Gravy
served with Butterbean Mash, Cabbage Timbale and Henderson's Syrup

To Serve 2
Ingredients

Marinade
4 tablespoons Henderson's Relish
1 glass red wine
2 cloves chopped garlic
1 large sprig thyme
1 large sprig rosemary
Salt & freshly-ground pepper

2 rabbit legs
1/2 pint (300ml) rabbit stock
(or brown chicken stock)
1 stick celery chopped
1/2 small onion chopped

Loin of Rabbit
2 loins of rabbit approximately 4–5oz
    (125–150g) in weight
8oz (250g) thinly sliced white onions
Salt & pepper
4 large sage leaves (do not chop)
3/4 pint (400ml) white chicken stock
1oz (25g) lard
1 teaspoon cornflour

Butterbean Mash
1 14oz (400g) tin butterbeans
1oz (25g) melted butter
Salt & pepper
2 tablespoons double cream

Cabbage Timbale
2 large Savoy cabbage leaves
    blanched and refreshed
2oz (50g) smoked bacon chopped
1 shallot, chopped
1oz (25g) butter
8oz (250g) finely shredded Savoy
    cabbage
Henderson's Relish
Black pepper

Method

Marinade
Mix all the ingredients together for the marinade and marinate the rabbit legs and the loin for 24 hours, or at least overnight, to absorb the flavours.

Place the rabbit legs and the marinade in a small pan, along with the stock and vegetables, bring to the boil then reduce to a simmer. Cover and cook for approximately 45 minutes until the meat is tender.

Loin of Rabbit
Heat the lard in a pan and add the onions, cook until beginning to soften (they must not colour). Add the seasoned rabbit, sage and stock. Bring to the boil, then reduce heat to a simmer and cook for 30–40 minutes. The onions will be almost dissolved and the rabbit will be tender. Remove the rabbit and keep it hot. Skim the fat from the surface of the gravy and remove the sage leaves. Mix the cornflour with a little cold water to a creamy consistency and add enough of the mix to thicken the gravy. Keep the gravy warm.

Butterbean Mash
Drain the beans then heat in the melted butter until thoroughly heated through. Then mash until smooth using a potato masher or a food processor. Add the cream and seasoning and keep warm until needed.

Cabbage Timbale
Use the cabbage leaves to line two buttered dariole moulds (or 2 individual steamed pudding dishes).

Melt the butter in a large frying pan and cook the shallot and the bacon until crisp and brown. Reduce the heat slightly and add the shredded cabbage, stirring all the time. Cook for only 3–4 minutes so the cabbage is still nice and green. Season with the Henderson's and black pepper. Set aside.

Meanwhile, remove the rabbit legs from the liquor, replace the liquor on the stove and reduce to a syrupy glaze. Strain and keep warm for service.

Strip the meat from the legs of the rabbit and discard the bones. Shred the rabbit meat and keep warm.

Fill one-third of the lined dariole mould with some of the cabbage leaves, then some of the shredded leg meat to two-thirds full. Finish off with the pan-fried cabbage, tuck in the lining leaves to seal well. Heat through quickly to keep bright green colour.

To Serve

Place the Butterbean Mash to one side of the plate and top with the Loin of Rabbit. Turn out the Cabbage Timbale and place to the opposite side of the plate. Spoon the White Onion Gravy over the loin and allow to 'puddle' on the plate. Carefully dribble the Henderson's Syrup around the Cabbage Timbale.

Serve with baby carrots and a seasoned Yorkshire pudding (sage & onion).

Beauchief Hotel

Abbeydale Road South, Sheffield
Telephone 0114 262 0500

The Beauchief Hotel, which dates back to 1885, has been a landmark on the A621 Bakewell road since Victorian times and the coming of the railway. It has a well established reputation for quality food and drink among the local community as well as with hotel guests.

The Restaurant, with its secluded areas for intimate dinners and special occasions, offers an excellent choice of traditional favourites or interesting new offerings from the à la carte and fixed-price menus. These include Pigeon and Rabbit Terrine, Braised Woodland Mushrooms, or Grilled Goat's Cheese on a French Brioche as starters, followed by tempting Medallion of Venison on a bed of Parsnip Purée with a rich Port Glace, a Saddle of Lamb stuffed with Kidneys and Herbs on a Red Wine Jus, or a Salmon Fondue filled with Scallops and served with a Butter Sauce.

General Manager, Craig Dowie, who joined the hotel team in July 1998, is keen to support Head Chef Colin McFarlane, in maintaining and improving the quality of the food, wine and service. Colin is a key member of the Regal Hotel Group's Food Development Team, sharing his skills and ideas with more than 100 sister hotels. It is reassuring to find traditional values at such reasonable prices in a restaurant which is well worth a visit.

Open   Monday–Saturday 7.00–10.00 p.m.
       Sunday 7.00–9.00 p.m.

Old Hamlet Forge Fillet Steak

by
Colin Mcfarlane
Head Chef at The Beauchief Hotel

Old Hamlet Forge Fillet Steak
Fillet of Beef and a Purée of Celeriac and Grilled Goat's Cheese
with Beef Confit Potatoes
Half Moon of Swede
Stuffed Courgette
Selection of Sauces, Basil, Veal Glace and the Marinade

To Serve 2
Ingredients

Marinade
- 4 teaspoons Henderson's Relish
- 2 measures Drambuie
- 2 glasses of red wine
- 2 shallots
- $1/2$ pepper
- 2 sprigs of thyme

Main Dish
- 2 x 6oz (170g) fillet steaks
- 2 slices of goat's cheese
- 1 small celeriac
- 1 small swede
- 2 small courgettes

- 1 carrot
- 1 beetroot
- 1 tomato
- 1 leek
- 2 medium potatoes
- 6 cèpes (or other mushrooms)
- Beef dripping
- Henderson's Relish
- Fresh basil
- 2 tablespoons olive oil
- $1/2$ clove garlic
- $1/2$ pint (300ml) of veal stock
- Salt & pepper

Method

Marinade

Sauté the shallots and pepper together until they start to caramelise, then add the red wine, Drambuie and Henderson's Relish and bring to the boil. Pass through a strainer into a small bowl, then add the steaks and leave for 24 hours to marinate.

Main Dish

Slice the tomato into 6 thin slices, then cut the cooked beetroot into 2 slices and leave in a warm place to dry out.

Peel and cut the celeriac into small pieces then boil. When cooked, purée and add salt and pepper.

Blanch the green leaves of the leek in hot water and refresh straight away in cold water. Repeat the same process for the carrot.

Line a small ring mould with the leaves of the leek and add the celeriac purée and keep warm.

Peel the swede and cut into half-moon shapes about $1/4''$ (.5cm) thick.

Core the courgettes with an apple corer and fill with the blanched carrot.

Cut the potatoes into 6 discs approximately $1/2''$ thick by $1 1/2''$ diameter (1cm x 3cm) using a pastry cutter. Cook in the beef fat and two tablespoons Henderson's Relish.

Take the 2 steaks out of the marinade and fry off. Cook the two steaks, preferably in a Chargrill, until cooked to your liking.

Blanch the swede in a pan of hot water until tender.

Sauces

Veal Glace

Reduce the $1/2$ pint of veal stock rapidly by two-thirds.

Marinade

Strain the marinade into a small sauce pan and reduce by two-thirds.

Basil

Liquidise the olive oil, basil and garlic and season well.

To Serve

Place the mould of celeriac and leek onto the centre of the plate with a slice of goat's cheese on top. Place 3 of the Beef Confit Potatoes evenly around the edge of the plate then put into a warm oven until the cheese starts to melt.

Remove the plate from the oven and place the Half Moons of Swede and a sliced Stuffed Courgette around the Goat's Cheese and top with 1 slice of the dried beetroot. Place a slice of the dried tomato on top of each of the potatoes.

To finish, pour the 3 Sauces (Basil, Reduction of Marinade, and the Veal Glace) evenly around the edge of the plate.

Manor House Hotel and Restaurant

10–15 High Street, Old Dronfield, Derbyshire
Telephone 01246 413971

Owners: Janet and Andrew Coghlan   Chef: Simon Lilley

Situated in the heart of Old Dronfield, the Manor House offers a professional, yet relaxed environment for both business and social travellers.

Combining the experience of 5 star hotel management with a personal and friendly touch, a unique and very special atmosphere is created.

There are two suites and eight en suite bedrooms combining high standards of modern luxury with the charm and ambience of a building dating from 1540. The Piper-Heidsieck suite is a new addition to the hotel facilities. This opulently restored suite is designed to reflect Piper's long standing relationship with the stars on the big screen and includes complimentary Champagne Piper. Oak beams and Derbyshire stone are features carried throughout the building.

The restaurant now enjoys an enviable reputation in the locality, serving new English classical cooking with influences from Europe and the Americas. Innovation of ideas and a light touch with sauces coupled with simple yet effective presentation of dishes ensure that the restaurant is often booked some weeks in advance and booking is recommended for weekend visits. Wines are treated with as much importance as food and the cellar is stocked with over 200 bins including wines form Schloss Reinhartshausen and the Millennium Collection.

Recommended by Johannsens™ this restaurant is a must for all those who appreciate good food.

A chauffeur service, using a Rolls Royce, is offered for local evening diners, enabling full enjoyment of a special night out, also available for residents and international guests, airport and railway station collection can be arranged (subject to booking).

Places of interest nearby include Chatsworth House, Haddon Hall, Bakewell and the Peak District, Blue John Mines, Chesterfield Spire and Dronfield Church.

Directions
Old Dronfield is three miles south of Sheffield, off the A61. The Manor House is in the centre of the village near the church.

Open 7 days a week 7.00–9.15 p.m.

Henderson's Pork Salsa

by
Simon Lilley
Head Chef at The Manor House Restaurant

Henderson's Pork Salsa

To Serve 2
Ingredients

1 English pork fillet
6 wonton pastry sheets
4oz (100g) local black pudding
1oz (25g) breadcrumbs
3 tablespoons Henderson's Relish
1 egg (for egg wash)
$1/2$ tablespoon virgin olive oil
6 plum cherry tomatoes

1 red onion
1 yellow pepper
1 green chilli
10 sundried tomatoes in 2 tablespoons olive oil
1 clove garlic
1 bunch coriander (fresh)
2 sprigs red basil
Salt & pepper

Method

Salsa
Finely dice the red onion, yellow pepper, green chilli and sundried tomatoes, ensuring you remove all seeds, add crushed garlic. Combine these together with the 2 tablespoons of olive oil from the sundried tomatoes and 2 tablespoons of Henderson's Relish. Add $1/2$ tablespoon of chopped coriander and adjust seasoning with salt and pepper. The salsa is now ready and can be left on one side.

Tomatoes
Next take the cherry tomatoes, slice off the tops and remove the seeds and trim the bases so they are able to rest upright. Fill with a little salsa and place on a non-stick baking tray.

Wontons
Blend the black pudding in a food processor and add 1 tablespoon of Henderson's Relish and the bread crumbs. The mixture should form a smooth paste. Add salt and pepper to taste.

Lay out the wonton sheets on a clean surface and brush with egg wash. Place a heaped teaspoon of the black pudding mix in the centre of each sheet and fold the pastry on a diagonal to form a triangle, seal the edges together by pinching. Place to one side.

The Pork

Using a sharp knife, trim and remove all the sinew from the pork fillet leaving the flesh intact and undamaged. Cut the pork into 2 equal portions. Heat $1/_2$ tablespoon of olive oil in a frying pan, season the pork with salt and pepper and place in the hot pan to seal and colour the meat on all sides. Once the meat is sealed place the frying pan into the oven if it is suitable (or transfer to a heated casserole or roasting tin) and cook for 10 minutes at 200°c (gas 6). This will leave the meat pink in the centre. Cook for longer if preferred.

While the pork is cooking. Warm the rest of the salsa dressing on a low heat. Do not boil.

Deep fry the wontons (180°C in a fryer) and cook until golden brown (approximately 1 minute). Remove and drain on kitchen paper.

Place the cherry tomatoes on the top shelf of the oven for the last 4 minutes of cooking time.

Deep fry the red basil for 10 seconds, remove and drain.

Remove the pork, allow to rest and remove the cherry tomatoes from the oven.

To Serve

Drizzle the salsa around the edge of the plate centre. Place the drained wontons and roasted tomatoes alternately next to the salsa. Slice the pork thinly and arrange, overlapping, in the centre of the plate. Decorate with the deep-fried red basil.

The Sheffield College

Granville Road
Telephone 0114 260 2060

As the largest College of Further Education in Europe, The Sheffield College offers an exciting and far reaching range of options, drawing on the skills and expertise of a large teaching staff from a broad background of academic and professional disciplines.

The College's catering and hospitality division, which is based in the School of Business, Leisure and Hospitality, is run by a team of professionals who regularly win awards and competitions and actively encourage their students to stretch themselves to reach their full potential.

The Sheffield College's catering programmes have both a national and international reputation for the quality of training they give to students. After completing courses at The Sheffield College, former students have gone on to build highly successful careers in hospitality, catering and hotel management, which have taken them to some of the best hotels, restaurants and kitchens around the globe.

Alongside the full-time and part-time catering provision for school leavers, The Sheffield College runs a wide range of specialist courses in catering, restaurant and bar-management skills.

The Sheffield College's restaurant, Minstrel's, has earned an enviable reputation in the City of Sheffield. Minstrel's is the place where the chefs and restaurateurs of the future have the chance to demonstrate their professional skills to the public, putting their new training under the closest scrutiny, all discreetly overseen by their tutors. Diners have the chance to sample a range of excellent menus at a fraction of the cost one would expect to pay in a commercial restaurant, all created and served by people who really care about getting it right. Such is the popularity of Minstrel's that it is often booked for both lunch and dinner far in advance.

The Sheffield College is proud of its hard-earned reputation for innovative training and teaching in the catering area. It continues to launch many new careers in this vibrant industry that offers travel world-wide and excellent employment opportunities.

| Open | Lunch | Tuesday–Friday | 12.30–3.00 p.m. |
| | Evening | Wednesday–Friday | 6.30–9.30 p.m. |

Students at work in The Sheffield College's training restaurant, Minstrel's.

The 1998 team of Sheffield College lecturers

Mike Morphew, **Divisional Manager of Hospitality and Catering**

Mike trained at Westminster College in the late 1960s. He went on to the Savoy and worked through all the parties (sections) in the kitchen. A move to the Connaught for a two-year spell proved to be extremely beneficial, as this furthered his career more than any other experience resulting in a six month spell at Buckingham Palace, followed by a six month period in Zurich.

John Janiszewski with Mike Morphew

On returning to Britain, Mike took up a position as the youngest Trust House Forte Head Chef at the age of 19. He moved on to other Head Chef and executive Chef positions before opening his own restaurant, firstly in Bath and then another in Dorset.

In 1984 he moved into education and is now Divisional Manager of Hospitality and Catering at The Sheffield College.

Mike has gained numerous awards at Hotelympia and other salons and has been part of the team of Chef Judges at local salons and Hotelympia.

A Relish of Beef
with
Henderson's Dumplings

To Serve 4
Ingredients

1½ lbs (750g) fillet of beef
2 shallots finely chopped
2 tablespoons of Henderson's Relish
½ pint (300ml) double cream
1 measure of brandy
1 lemon

1 teaspoon of chopped parsley, tarragon and
  chervil
¼ pint (150ml) of raw choux pastry mix
1 tablespoon olive oil
1oz butter
Salt & black pepper

Method

Marinade
Cut the beef into 1″ x ½″ (2cm x 1cm) strips then place them into a bowl. Season and sprinkle with 1 tablespoon of Henderson's Relish to marinate.

Dumplings
Mix all the chopped herbs and the remainder of the Henderson's into the choux pastry. Put the mixture into a piping bag.

Place a shallow pan on the stove filled with simmering water, pipe and cut small sections of the pastry into the water and allow to simmer (these will puff up like small soufflés). When light in consistency, refresh in cold water and keep for use later.

The Beef
Heat a little olive oil and butter in a sauté pan, add the chopped shallot and fry gently, then add the fillet of beef and fry quickly until cooked (approximately 2–3 minutes), remove from the pan and keep warm.

Add a knob of butter to the pan and heat until foaming, add the brandy and ignite in the pan, add the cream and boil rapidly. Season well and add the lemon juice.

In a separate pan toss the drained dumplings in a little butter to glaze them.

Add the meat back to the cream sauce but do not boil, place the dumplings on top and serve immediately with a wild rice pilaff.

Griddled King Scallops
with Crispy Chinese Vegetables, Caramelised Sesame Pecans and a Lime & Lemon Grass Sauce

To Serve 2
Ingredients

10 king scallops (cleaned)
1 x 2″ (5cm) piece of mooli, peeled and sliced
6 spring onions, sliced
16 broad beans, blanched and peeled
16 snow peas, sliced obliquely
2 baby pak choi, stems sliced, leaves torn
6 asparagus, sliced obliquely
$1/2$ yellow pepper, sliced obliquely
$1/2$ red chilli, finely chopped
1 stem lemon grass, inner part finely sliced
1 piece stem ginger, cut into julienne
Juice of 1 lime
1 tablespoon sesame oil
1 tablespoon olive oil

2 tablespoons Henderson's Relish
Dash of light soy sauce
1 crushed garlic clove
Freshly ground salt & black pepper

Dressing for Scallops
Finely grated zest of 1 lime
Juice of 1 lime
3 teaspoons ginger syrup from stem ginger
1 tablespoon olive oil

Caramelised Pecans
10 pecan nuts
3 teaspoons icing sugar
1 tablespoon toasted sesame seeds

Method

Preheat oven to 220°C (Gas 7), gently heat wok to all over even heat and heat griddle or skillet.

Prepare all ingredients.

Caramelised nuts
Heat icing sugar, with the pecans, in a frying pan over a gentle heat until it melts to form a caramel swirl to coat. Remove to a baking parchment and sprinkle with sesame seeds. Allow to cool and crisp.

Scallops
Griddle scallops until golden on one side. Remove and sit on oven tray golden side up. Drizzle dressing over. Heat for 1 minute ONLY in oven until hot.

Vegetables
Add oil to wok and stir-fry all vegetables. Start with chilli, lemon grass, garlic and asparagus then add rest of vegetables and seasonings. Taste and adjust. Stir in nuts and finally scallops.

Serve in a pretty dish.

Roast Chicken with a stuffing of Spinach, Feta and Olives flavoured with Henderson's Relish

Served with a Red Wine, Thyme & Shallot Sauce and toasted Pine Nuts

To serve 4

Ingredients

1 roasting chicken approximately 3 lbs (1.5kg)
1 pint chicken stock
2 dessertspoons of Henderson's Relish
3oz (75g) fresh spinach
1 small clove of garlic
4oz (100g) feta cheese
1oz (25g) butter
1 dessertspoon vegetable oil

1 dessertspoon plain flour
1 tablespoon pine nuts
Fresh thyme
1 small glass of red wine
2 shallots
Black pepper
12 black olives, preserved in oil if possible
String to tie

Method

Skin the chicken by making an incision in the skin along the full length of the back (base of the chicken). Use a small knife and your fingers to ease away the skin, cut the skin only to remove it from the tips of the legs and wings, and again to remove from around the parson's nose.

Now remove the two breasts from the bone, and also the two legs, to end up with four boneless pieces of meat. (Place the skin and chicken pieces in the fridge until the stuffing is ready).

You could ask your butcher to prepare the chicken for you.

Place the carcass in a large pan and cover with cold water, bring to the boil then simmer for 2–3 hours to make a simple stock.

Melt half of the butter slowly in a large sauce pan, add the peeled crushed garlic clove and cook gently for one minute. Turn up the heat and add the washed spinach, cook until just fallen, then place in a colander to drain and cool.

Cut up the feta into a small dice and sprinkle with half of the Henderson's Relish. Stone and cut into small pieces 8 of the olives, mix these gently with the cooled spinach and the cheese.

To Assemble the Chicken

Spread out the chicken skin on a board outer side down. Place on this the 2 breasts, which have been cut lengthways and opened out, season these with a little ground black pepper.

Place the stuffing in a line down the centre of the breasts, then top with the boneless leg meat and season again with a little black pepper. Wrap the skin round to form a neat chicken joint, turn over, to put the folded side underneath, then tie loosely with string in 5 or 6 places.

Brush with vegetable oil and place in a roasting tin. Cook in a pre-heated oven at 200 °C (gas 6) for approximately 50 minutes. (Turn the oven down to 160 °C (gas 3) if the chicken starts to become too brown.) Allow to rest, covered, for 15 minutes.

Sauce

Reduce the chicken stock by half, then add the finely chopped shallots, half a teaspoon of chopped fresh thyme, the red wine and remaining Relish. Simmer this for 5 minutes and then thicken slightly with a paste made from the remaining butter and flour— whisk this in a little at a time into the boiling liquid. Finally, check the seasoning and add the remaining finely chopped olives. Keep the sauce warm.

To Serve

Carve the chicken into thick slices, sprinkle with the pine nuts and coat with the sauce, garnish with sprigs of fresh thyme.

Sautéed Foie Gras
Pan Fried Bubble & Squeak Cake, Shallot-Thyme Jam, Home-made Gravy

To Serve 4 as a first course
Ingredients

Foie Gras
4 x 4oz (100g) slices best foie gras
4 sprigs fresh thyme
Henderson's Relish to taste

Bubble & Squeak Cake
1lb (500g) potatoes, peeled and diced
1 Spanish onion, sliced
4 rashers smoked dry-cured bacon, shredded
2oz (50g) Brussels sprouts, shredded
4oz (125g) seasonal cabbage, shredded

1oz (25g) duck fat
1oz (25g) carrot, finely diced
1oz (25g) celeriac, finely diced
1oz (25g) swede, finely diced
Flour
Lard
Mace, salt, black pepper
Henderson's Relish to taste

Home-made Gravy
Your best gravy and Henderson's Relish

Shallot Jam
12 large shallots, thinly sliced
2 cloves garlic, crushed
1 bay leaf
1 sprig thyme
1oz (25g) duck fat
2oz (50g) brown sugar
2 tablespoons red wine
2 tablespoons balsamic vinegar
Salt, black pepper, Henderson's Relish to taste

Method

Bubble & Squeak Cake
Heat a large heavy-bottomed pan and add the duck fat, when hot add the onions and bacon and cook until golden brown. Deglaze the pan with a good dash of Henderson's Relish (pour in the Relish and lightly boil to lift the sediment). Add the remainder of the vegetables and season with salt and pepper. When all the items are cooked, deglaze the pan with more Henderson's Relish, correct the seasoning and leave to cool.

Place potatoes into a large pan of heavily salted water, cook the potatoes. When cooked, drain and then pass them through a fine sieve, the end result required is a dry smooth potato mash. Mix the mash and the cooked vegetables together, correct the seasoning, and then shape into scone-size rounds. Place in the fridge until required.

Shallot Jam
Heat the duck fat in a large heavy-bottomed pan, add shallots and cook until golden brown. Add the bay leaf, sprig of thyme, garlic, sugar, red wine, balsamic vinegar, seasonings and a good splash of Henderson's Relish to the cooked shallots. Cook for 60 minutes on a low heat until you have a good caramelised shallot jam, check for seasoning and taste.

Flavour your gravy with Henderson's Relish.

Flour the bubble and squeak cake and gently fry in a little lard until golden brown. Place the cake onto a baking sheet and bake for 5 minutes at 200°C (gas 6).

Warm the shallot jam and gravy.

Heat a non-stick pan, season the foie gras and add a sprig of thyme, sauté for 60 seconds per side. When the foie gras is cooked deglaze the pan with a good splash of Relish.

To Serve

Place the bubble and squeak cake onto a warm plate with the foie gras on the top and then a small amount of the shallot jam, pour the gravy around the outside of the cake and serve.

Fruit, Nut and Vegetable Pasty in Henderson's Relish Crust

by
Claire Firth
Head Chef at Tom Cobleigh's Waggon & Horses, Millhouses

Fruit, Nut and Vegetable Pasty
served with a Rich Mushroom & Sherry Sauce
Accompaniments: Filled Roasted Red Onion with Potato, Pear & Leek Purée, Glazed
Baby Turnips, Carrot Rings, Sautéed Batons of Cucumber, Baby Corn Cobs

To Serve 2. This dish is suitable for vegetarians.

Ingredients

Pastry
- 8oz (250g) self-raising flour
- 4oz (125g) solid vegetable fat or vegetable margarine
- 6–8 tablespoons of Henderson's Relish
- Beaten egg yolk and salt to glaze

Filling
- 1 tablespoon of olive oil
- 2 tomatoes, chopped
- 2 medium courgettes, chopped
- 1 small parsnip, finely chopped
- 1 medium onion, chopped
- 4oz (125g) button mushrooms, chopped
- 2 tablespoons crunchy peanut butter
- 2 tablespoons cranberry jelly
- or
- 4oz (125g) fresh cranberries and a little sugar
- 6 spring onions
- $1/4$ pint (100ml) single cream
- 2 tablespoons of tomato purée
- 2 tablespoons of Henderson's Relish
- Marjoram
- Chopped parsley to taste
- Thyme
- Salt & pepper

Wild Mushroom Sauce

For the Stock
- Potato
- Carrot
- Onion
- Celery
- Bay leaf
- $2^{1}/_{2}$ pints (1.5 litres) of water
- 1 tablespoon of olive oil

The Sauce
- 1 pint (600ml) of vegetable stock
- Cream & Relish to taste
- 1 oz (25g) of butter
- 8 oz (250g) button mushrooms
- 4 oz (125g) oyster mushrooms
- 4 teaspoons flour
- 1 measure sweet sherry
- Salt & pepper

Filled Onion
- 2 large potatoes
- 2 medium red onions
- 2 dessert pears
- 1 large leek
- Salt & pepper
- A little olive oil

Vegetables
- $1/2$ cucumber
- 1 pack baby corn cobs
- Chives
- 2 carrots
- 4 small turnips

Method

Pastry

Sieve flour and salt into a bowl and add small pieces of chilled fat. Rub lightly together until the mixture resembles fine breadcrumbs. Next add the chilled Henderson's Relish and mix to form a smooth dough. Leave pastry to rest in fridge until the filling is prepared and cooked.

Filling

For the pasty filling any combination of vegetables can be used but this combination is just about the right mix between fibrous and soft vegetables. Using the peanut sauce and the cranberries adds a touch of sweetness which works perfectly with the Relish in the crust.

Sweat the onions in oil. Prepare all the vegetables and add to the pan along with the herbs, cook until just soft. Add the purée and Relish, correct the seasoning and leave to cool.

Peanut Sauce

Sauté the spring onion in small amount of oil, then add the peanut butter. Stir in cream to make a fairly thick sauce.

Shape and fill the pasty and top with the peanut sauce and cranberries. Bake in a moderate oven for 45 minutes or until golden and crispy.

Wild Mushroom Sauce

Vegetable Stock

Scrub then roughly chop a selection of vegetables. Fry off all vegetables gently, add water and simmer for 1½–2 hours in a covered pan.

Sauce

Cook button mushrooms in butter over a high heat for 2 minutes, add sherry and reduce. Lower the heat, add flour and cook for 3-4 minutes. Gradually add stock stirring constantly and allow to simmer. Season then liquidise until smooth.

Sauté the oyster mushrooms then add to the smooth sauce. Reheat, gently adding cream and Relish.

Filled Onion

Slice top and bottom off the onion so it stands upright, sprinkle with olive oil and season. Cover with foil and roast in a hot oven for 20 minutes.

Meanwhile, peel potatoes, leek and pears, chop, then boil until soft. Mash with the cream and butter and season to taste.

Remove onion from oven, allow to cool then peel and scoop out the middle. Fill with the potato mixture, replace the onion top. Reheat when needed.

For the Vegetables

Baton the cucumber removing the seeds, then sauté together with the baby corn cobs in a little olive oil and butter. Arrange in bundles and tie with softened chive.

Slice the carrots into chunky rings then cook in water and a little butter in a covered pan.

Trim the turnips leaving a little stalk on each and wash them. Put in a small pan with a little sugar, butter and seasoning, boil then cook gently until tender. When almost cooked remove lid and boil rapidly to reduce liquid to glaze.

Being born and bred in Sheffield, Henderson's was always on the table when I was a child so I learnt of its qualities at an early age. It has become an irreplaceable ingredient in many of my recipes.

Crab and Avocado Risotto

Ingredients

8oz (250g) cooked white crab meat
2 ripe avocados, peeled and diced
1 medium onion, peeled and finely chopped
10oz (300g) Arborio rice
1 tablespoon chopped garlic

2 tablespoons Henderson's Relish
2 pints (1 litre) vegetable stock
1oz (25g) butter
2oz (50g) freshly grated Parmesan
Chopped flat leaf parsley to garnish

Method

Heat the stock and allow to simmer. Soften the onion and garlic in a heavy-bottomed pan in a little olive oil then add the rice and coat well. Slowly add the simmering stock, about $1/4$ of a pint at a time, stirring constantly. Allow the stock to be absorbed before adding more (the more stock you add, the creamier the risotto).

When the rice is cooked, it should be firm to bite (or al dente) stir in the crab, avocado and Henderson's and mix well. Cover the pan and allow to stand for a few minutes to allow it to absorb any remaining liquid. Season to taste and stir in the butter and Parmesan. Serve immediately with chopped parsley to garnish.

Roast Salmon with Henderson's & Horseradish Cream

Ingredients

4 x 6–8oz (175–250g) salmon steaks, skinned
1 teaspoon coarse sea salt
Freshly ground black pepper
1 tablespoon chopped dill
A squeeze of lemon juice

For the Cream
2oz (50g) freshly grated horseradish
2 tablespoons Henderson's Relish
$1/4$ pint (150ml) whipping cream
2 tablespoons chopped mint
Pinch of salt

Method

Salmon
Preheat the oven to 180°C (gas 4).

Place the salmon steaks in a lightly oiled roasting tin and sprinkle with salt, pepper, dill and lemon juice. Cook in the oven for 15–20 minutes or until just cooked (it should be opaque and tender).

Cream
Put all the ingredients in a whisking bowl and whisk till your arm hurts—or until you have stiff peaks.

To Serve

Place the salmon on the centre of the plate with a good dollop of cream on top. Serve immediately as the cream will start to melt.

A nice accompaniment is steamed broccoli and new potatoes.

Nonna's Ristorante

539 Ecclesall Road, Sheffield
Telephone 0114 268 6166

When 80-year-old Andrina Decol-Grazi opened a traditional deli in Modena, Italy, in the 50s, she never thought an English version would be opening in her name almost 50 years later. That's exactly what happened when grandson Gian, together with lifelong friend Maurizio, decided to open an up-to-date version on Sheffield's fashionable Ecclesall Road.

Gian was so impressed by his grandmother's thriving business that the Sheffield version is named Nonna's Deli, Espresso Bar & Restaurant—Nonna is Italian for granny.

That was two years ago. It has continued to go from strength to strength, incorporating three ideas under one roof. The Deli, serving only genuine Italian products, including Nonna's own exclusive range of products, pasta, olive oil and biscotti. The Espresso Bar, serving the finest cappuccinos and espressos with Italian television in the background and even *La Gazzetta* giornale to provide the true atmosphere of Italy. Thirdly, the Ristorante, styled like a Tuscan terrazzo, with faded photos of *La Famiglia* adorning the walls. It runs two menus, a lighter daytime menu, with bruschetta, crostini, premier fresh pasta etc, whereas the evening menu, which has gained in reputation, is more à la carte.

The combined talents and family history of Maurizio Mori and Gian Bohan provide the foundations of this quality and unique establishment.

Further background information is available, why not visit our website?
http://welcome.to/nonnas.

Open   Sunday   11.00 a.m.–5.00 p.m.
      Monday   8.00 a.m.–7.00 p.m.
      Tuesday–Saturday   8.00 a.m.–9.45 p.m.

Filetto Alla Boscaiola

by

W. Severn & S. Berry

Head Chefs at Nonna's Ristorante

Filetto Alla Boscaiola

To Serve 2
Ingredients

Steak Marinade
5 tablespoons of Henderson's Relish
5 tablespoons of olive oil
Salt & pepper
2 x 5–6oz (150–175g) fillet steaks
6oz (175g) wild mushrooms

Spinach Stuffing
6 nuggets of frozen spinach
$1/2$ clove garlic, crushed
1 dessertspoon of oil
1 dessertspoon of double cream
Salt & pepper
1 small egg

Pepper Sauce
$1/4$ small onion, diced
2 red peppers, diced
1 beef tomato, diced
1 cup of water or stock
1 clove of garlic, crushed

Polenta
2 cups of water
1 cup of polenta flour
Butter
1 dessertspoon of basil pesto
1oz (20g) of Parmesan cheese
1 grilled aubergine
Sundried tomato paste

Potatoes
2 large potatoes, peeled
6 rosemary stems
2 cloves garlic, crushed
Knob of butter
Oil
Salt & pepper

Method

Steak Marinade
The night before, mix the ingredients for the marinade and place in a dish with the steak.

Spinach Stuffing
Fry the frozen spinach in a dessertspoon of oil with $1/2$ clove crushed garlic until defrosted and water has evaporated. Beat a small egg together with a dessertspoon of cream. Stir into the spinach quickly, add seasoning and leave to cool.

The Steak
Remove the steak from the marinade and cut out a small circle in the steak and fill with the spinach mix. Place on a baking tray, spoon a little of the marinade on top and season. The steak will take 12 minutes to cook, rare, 200°C (gas 6). Cut in half before serving to reveal the centre with spinach stuffing.

Pepper Sauce
Fry onion, peppers and garlic in a little oil for 2 minutes. Add the diced beef tomatoes and cup of water, cook until peppers are soft. Pass through food mill. Check seasoning.

Polenta Tricolore
Put 2 cups of water & about 1oz (30g) of butter in a sauce pan with a pinch of salt and pepper. Bring to the boil and whisk in the polenta flour, cook for 5 minutes over a low heat. Take off heat and divide into three containers. Add 1 dessertspoon of basil pesto to one, and 1 dessertspoon of sun dried tomato paste to another and, finally, add a spoon of grated Parmesan to the last container. Using a mould, layer the tricolore polenta into a tower using the aubergine slices between each layer.

Potatoes
Peel the potatoes then use a melon baller to make 24 balls, put in a frying pan with 1 dessertspoon of butter and 1 of oil, the crushed garlic and the stripped stalks of rosemary. Cook slowly until light brown and soft, add salt and pepper. Cool, then thread 4 balls onto each rosemary stick. Serve 3 sticks per person.

The potatoes and polenta tower will take about 5 minutes, so put them in the oven to warm 5 minutes before the steak is cooked.
or
The potatoes, polenta and sauce can be made beforehand and warmed when needed.

Just before you are ready to serve, heat the rest of the marinade in a large sauté pan and fry the mushrooms. Drizzle some of the marinade oil onto the red pepper sauce and the steak.

Roast Loin of Lamb

stuffed with Sundried Tomatoes, Olives and Herbs on a bed of Artichoke, Potato & Tomato Confit with a Port & Thyme Jus

To Serve 2
Ingredients

1 loin of lamb, boned
2oz (50g) sundried tomatoes
20 black olives, pitted
1 tablespoon oregano
1 tablespoon parsley
1 clove garlic

4 artichoke hearts
2 tomatoes, peeled pipped & diced
  (tomato concassé)
1 potato
1oz (25g) duck fat
1 tablespoon fresh thyme

2 shallots
1 glass port
1 glass white wine
$1/2$ pint (300ml) thickened stock (jus)
3oz (75g) butter
1 tablespoon Henderson's Relish
Salt & pepper

Method

Chop the sundried tomatoes and mix with 1 clove of crushed garlic, parsley and oregano and half of the olives. Add salt and pepper and 1 tablespoon of Henderson's Relish.

Trim off excess fat from the lamb, leaving the edge of the meat with enough covering of fat to fold around and protect the meat. Smear the tomato mixture on the meat, fold the fat round and tie up. Leave to rest, then roast in a hot oven.

Dice the potato and blanch in boiling water to par-cook. Refresh and dry.

Melt the duck fat until hot, add the potatoes, diced artichoke heart, tomato concassé and clove of crushed garlic. Season and cook to reduce excess liquor.

Chop shallots then sweat in butter but do not colour. Add chopped thyme and sauté for 1 minute. Add port, wine and reduce. Add Jus. Reduce by $1/4$ and add butter.

To Serve

Take out the lamb and allow it to rest for 5 minutes.
Place mixture of artichoke in the middle of the plate. Cut two thick slices of lamb and lay them on top of the mixture, then pour over sauce and finally decorate with the remaining olives.

Brian Turner

Pan Fried Escalope of Salmon

by
Sean Wallis
at Stakis Sheffield

Stakis Sheffield

North Quay, Victoria Quays, Furnival Road, Sheffield
Telephone 0114 252 5500

Sheffield is a city on the up. Increasingly recognised as the national centre for sports, it has tremendous football, rugby and athletics facilities, and some great local golf courses. Even your hotel caters for the sports enthusiast, with its 20m swimming pool and magnificent gymnasium.

As you explore the Peak District, make sure you visit Chatsworth House. It has fabulous gardens and is possibly the best Stately Home in England. For a trip with a difference, head underground through the Blue John mine and other caverns at Castleton. Of course, you might prefer to spend a day at Meadowhall, one of Europe's largest shopping centres. Alternatively, wander along the quayside by the hotel and admire the painted barges. Afterwards, relax with a drink in the Italian-style Espresso bar or sit on the terrace. Then you can enjoy the excellent food in Bar Bacoa, a lively, barbecue-style restaurant, where you can actually watch the chefs prepare your food.

About the Hotel
Delightful waterside location • 128 bedrooms
• Terrace overlooking the quayside
• 23 hour room service • Lifts • Laundry service available • Free car park • Bar Bacoa barbecue restaurant and Espresso bar • Private terrace area

Hotel Leisure Facilities
20m Indoor Heated Swimming Pool • Sauna
• Steam Room • Solarium • Whirlpool Spa
• Fully equipped Gymnasium • Virtual Reality Equipment • Aerobics Studio • Beauty Suites
• Hairdressers

| Restaurant open | Lunch | Sunday–Friday | 12.30–2.00 p.m. |
| | Evenings | Every day | 7.00–9.30 p.m. |

Pan Fried Escalope of Salmon
with Henderson's Crispy Dill Noodles married with Braised Baby Fennel and Butter Sauce

To Serve 2
Ingredients

2 x 6oz (175g) escalopes (thinly-sliced fillets) of salmon
6oz (175g) plain strong flour
1 egg and egg yolk
2 tablespoons of oil, plus oil for frying
6-8 heads of baby fennel
Bunch of fresh dill

Leaves of heart of curly endive
Leaves of cornmanche (lamb's lettuce)
3 cherry tomatoes
3/4 pint (450ml) of good fish stock
Unsalted butter
Salt & black pepper
1 dessertspoon Henderson's Relish

Method

Add the egg, oil and salt to the sieved flour and mix together to form a soft dough to make the noodles. Add some chopped dill and Henderson's Relish, knead the dough and allow to rest, covered, in the fridge.

Roll the dough out to form thin sheets and cut into noodles with a cutting roller (thinnest setting on a pasta roller). Cook the noodles in salted water with a little oil for 3 minutes, drain off and place in a frying pan with a little oil in a pastry ring and fry until crisp on one side.

Braise the fennel until cooked. Lightly grill the cherry tomatoes.

The Sauce
Reduce the fish stock by 2/3 until a thick consistency. Finish by adding cold unsalted butter cubes and whisking in Henderson's Relish, and then season as required.

Spoon the noodles onto the plate crispy side up.

Fry the salmon, skin side down first then turn over until cooked, and place on top of the noodles. Decorate with endive, grilled cherry tomatoes, cornmanche and braised fennel.

Rack of Lamb

by
Simon Harris
Head Chef at the Moat House, Sheffield

Rack of Lamb
with a Chick Pea Rosti and Provençale Vegetables

To Serve 2
Ingredients

2 x 7-bone rack of lamb (French trimmed)
4oz (125g) fresh breadcrumbs
2 tablespoons butter
1 sprig rosemary
1 clove garlic
4 tablespoons Henderson's Relish

Rosti
2 medium potatoes
1 tin chick peas
$1/2$ teaspoon cumin
Salt & pepper

Vegetables
$1/2$ teaspoon finely-sliced fresh ginger
1 sprig coriander
1 finely-diced courgette
1 finely-diced pepper (mixed colours look nice)
4 mushrooms, quartered
1 oyster mushroom, sliced
1 tablespoon Henderson's Relish
1 sprig mint
1 pinch saffron
$1/4$ pint (150ml) vegetable stock
$1/8$ pint (75ml) white wine
1 tablespoon olive oil

Method

Trim all the fat off the lamb leaving just the eye of the meat. Season and marinate in the Henderson's Relish together with half of the rosemary for 30 minutes.

Blend the remainder of the rosemary, garlic and bread in a food processor. Lightly fry this mixture in the butter until lightly crisped.

Spread the breadcrumbs onto the back of the lamb ensuring it is firmly pressed on. Place the lamb on a baking sheet and roast for approximately 30 minutes at 200°C (gas 6).

Rosti
Peel and grate the potatoes, roughly chop the chick peas, add cumin, season and mix all the ingredients together.

Shape into 2 circles and pan fry gently until crisp on the outside and cooked all the way through.

Vegetables
Sweat the courgettes, peppers and mushrooms in the oil. Add the saffron and ginger, then the wine and stock and reduce by half. Just before serving add the chopped coriander and mint as well as the Henderson's Relish and adjust the seasoning if necessary.

To Serve

Remove the lamb from the oven, slice into cutlets and arrange on top of the rosti, surround with the Provençale vegetables.

Santino's Ristorante Italiano

371–373 Ecclesall Road, Sheffield
Telephone 0114 267 0078

In June, 1993, the original Santino's Ristorante Italiano was born on Ecclesall Road. Owned and run by Nicolino and Tonino Dente, the small 35-seater restaurant quickly built up a reputation for good value Italian food served in a cosy traditional atmosphere.

The restaurant's popularity soon outstripped supply and, when the adjoining restaurant became available, Nick and Toni decided the time was right to expand. The two restaurants were initially run in tandem but, in October 1997, both restaurants were closed to carry out major modifications resulting in the Santino's you see today—an open and spacious 80-seat restaurant serving Italian and Continental cuisine.

Considerable effort has gone into retaining the Continental feel, with white walls, murals and painted vines making a bright and lively atmosphere. Some evenings when the place is really buzzing the waiters have been known to burst into song—Pavarotti style. The excellent food and service, the atmosphere and value for money have all resulted in Santino's being one of the most popular restaurants in Sheffield.

A full à la Carte menu is available, with all meals cooked to order so it is no problem to add to or remove items from your chosen dish. Santino's serves everything from pizzas to pastas, beef, poultry and fish dishes, as well as vegetarian and vegan options. Chalkboards display mouth-watering daily specials plus recommended wines. To finish off, there are tempting sweets such as pancakes, Toscanella and home made Tiramisu, or why not try some of the many flavours of traditional Italian ice cream from the gelateria.

Open   Lunch   Tuesday–Sunday   11.30 a.m.–3.00 p.m.
        Evenings   Monday–Friday   6.00–11.00 p.m., 12.00 p.m. Saturday & Sunday

Pette Di Anatra con Proscuitto e Mozzarella

by
Nicolino Dente
Head Chef at Santino's Ristorante Italiano

Pette Di Anatra con Proscuitto e Mozzarella
(Duck Breast with Parma Ham and Mozzarella)

To Serve 2

Ingredients

Henderson's Relish
2 medium sized duck breasts
Plain flour
2 eggs, size 3
Golden bread crumbs
Grated Parmesan cheese
Chopped basil
Chopped parsley
Olive oil

12oz (300g) fresh mozzarella cheese
Parma ham slices
Fresh whole herbs for garnish
Fresh lemon juice
6oz (175g) wild mushrooms
2 cloves of garlic
4oz (125g) butter
Mixed seasonal vegetables

Method

Marinate the duck breasts in olive oil, lemon and Henderson's Relish, preferably for 24 hours or overnight, and season.

Trim excess fat from the duck breasts and cut into four equal parts, slightly flatten using a meat hammer. Coat the duck pieces in seasoned flour, shaking off any excess, then dip first in beaten egg and then into a mix of the bread crumbs, Parmesan cheese and chopped herbs, shake off any excess.

Sauté the pieces of coated duck in butter until golden brown, drain any excess fat off using absorbent paper.

Slice the fresh mozzarella, place one piece of mozzarella then a slice of Parma ham onto each of the duck pieces. Place in a greased tray and grill until mozzarella is golden brown.

Sauté the cleaned wild mushrooms in garlic and butter.

Vegetables
Clean and cut vegetables to the required size, then blanch until crisp to bite. Drain whilst still hot, then sauté in garlic butter and herbs.

To Serve

Place the mushrooms on a plate and place golden brown pieces of duck onto the mushrooms, sprinkle with chopped herbs and serve with stir-fried vegetables.

Pan Fried Scallops

by
Wayne Bosworth
Head Chef at Rafters

Rafters

Oakbrook Road, Sheffield
Telephone 0114 230 4819

Rafters is situated upstairs on the corner of Oakbrook Road, Nethergreen and is fully licensed.

The dining area is an unusual hexagonal-shaped room with bricked walls and a modern contemporary curved bar, all warmly lit by hand-blown lighting from Milan, whilst the furnishings are in lemons and terracottas giving the restaurant a Mediterranean feel. It is a family-run business giving a friendly informal service which creates a pleasant and welcoming atmosphere.

Chefs Wayne and Jamie were both trained at Castle College in Sheffield. Wayne went on to work in Edinburgh for three years, the Savoy Hotel for three years and Odette's Restaurant, Regents Park, before returning to work in local hotels in Sheffield until he found Rafters. Jamie worked in London, France and Paul Heathcote's Brasserie before joining forces with Wayne to fulfil their ambition of running their own restaurant.

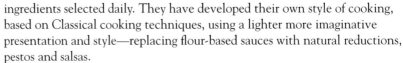

Award winning chefs, Wayne and Jamie, prepare the food from the best fresh ingredients selected daily. They have developed their own style of cooking, based on Classical cooking techniques, using a lighter more imaginative presentation and style—replacing flour-based sauces with natural reductions, pestos and salsas.

The menu is a set price of £21.50 for 3 courses. Everything on the menu is made on the premises, including the bread, ice creams and petits fours.

Open Monday, and Wednesday–Saturday evenings 7.00–10.00 p.m.—booking is advisable.

Pan Fried Scallops
with a Smoked Salmon, Rocket & Parmesan Salad
served with a Henderson's Salsa

To Serve 2
Ingredients

10 large fresh scallops
2oz (50g) salad rocket
1oz (25g) fresh Parmesan cheese
4 slices of smoked salmon
$1/4$ pint (100ml) olive oil
1 shallot

$1/3$ pint (200ml) Henderson's
1 clove garlic
1 sprig of fresh basil
3 tablespoons balsamic vinegar
1 jar sun dried tomato purée
2 large red potatoes

1 sprig fresh mint
1 sprig fresh coriander
1 sprig chervil
2 spring onions

Method

Marinade
Finely chop the shallot, crush the garlic and chop 2 basil leaves, place in a bowl and add 2 tablespoons of olive oil and 1 tablespoon of Henderson's Relish.
Place the scallops in the marinade for 10 minutes.

Caramel
Bring to the boil $1/3$ pint (200ml) of Henderson's Relish then add to this 3 tablespoons of balsamic vinegar and reduce by half to a slight caramel.

Potatoes
Wash, peel and cut the potatoes into chips and blanch for 3-4 minutes in the fryer (until partly cooked but not coloured) then drain.

Salsa
Chop the mint, chervil, coriander, basil and spring onions and add 1 teaspoon of the caramel. Add the chopped herbs to $1^{1}/_{2}$ tablespoons of olive oil and season with salt and pepper.

Salad
Wash and dry the rocket and cut the Parmesan into shavings. Season the salad with salt and cracked black pepper and add the Parmesan. Dress with olive oil and a drizzle of the caramel.

To Serve

Deep fry the chips in hot fat and serve on a side plate with Henderson's Relish.

Wrap the smoked salmon around the salad to form a wall. Place dots of sun dried tomato purée all around the plate. Place pools of salsa around the plate.

In a hot frying pan seal the scallops in a touch of olive oil for 1 minute each side—no longer.

Place the scallops on the plate and drizzle with the caramel.

TRADITIONAL DISHES

Brearley's

7–9 Langsett Road South, Oughtibridge
Telephone 0114 286 2261

Quickly gaining a reputation as one of Sheffield's most interesting restaurants, Brearley's opened its doors on the 1st February 1998. It is the realisation of an ambition of Stephen Brearley, who has switched roles from Marketing and Management, to that of Restaurateur.

Having 30 covers, Brearley's, in the centre of Oughtibridge Village, is warm, welcoming and cosy with an 'olde worlde' feel achieved by the clever use of stone, plaster and wooden beams. The staff are very efficient and attentive, and help to ensure that you feel welcome.

Affairs of the kitchen are more than capably taken care of by Jonathan Gillott, an extremely competent Chef, of National and International experience. Stephen says of Jonathan, 'I believe he is the best', and this is borne out by the large number of people who are devoted to his style, travelling for many miles to partake of his cuisine.

Living close by on a smallholding is very useful, as the kitchen garden has been extended enabling Brearley's clientele to enjoy the benefit of organically-grown potatoes, vegetables and herbs. Poultry and game birds will be reared from next spring.

Fish, of which there is a large range, is a speciality, as well as crabs, lobster, mussels, scallops and oysters. If fish is for you, Brearley's will be pleased to ensure provision of your favourite if you mention it when you book.

Steak, lamb, veal and chicken are a delight with Jonathan's special sauces—all home made of course. He also makes bread on the premises as well as ice cream.

Fifteen minutes by car from the centre of Sheffield, a journey once taken will be one you wish to repeat.

Open Sunday Lunch 12 noon–3 p.m.
Weekdays: Evenings 7 p.m.–Midnight. A La Carte–Table D'Hote
Lunch 12 noon–2.30 p.m.

Ye Olde Yorkshire Hash

This is a very simple but quite delicious warming dish for autumn or winter.
It also tastes just as good reheated, adding to its versatility,
surely a dish for which Henderson's Relish was created – and one
which has excellent nutritional values.

To Serve 4
Ingredients

$1^1/_2$ lbs (750g) stewing beef (shin, flank or skirt –
your butcher will cut it into medium sized cubes).
2 large onions
2 large carrots
2 sticks celery
4 large potatoes
2 tablespoons tomato concentrate

2 tablespoons plain flour
$1/_2$ pints (800ml) of brown stock
1 sprig of thyme
Henderson's Relish
2 bay leaves
Salt & pepper
1oz (25g) dripping

Method

Heat the dripping in a large pan or casserole dish.
Add the meat and brown on all sides, add the
chopped onions and cook for 5 minutes.

Add the tomato concentrate, then mix in the flour.
Pour in the stock along with herbs, salt and pepper
and leave to simmer for 30 minutes.

Add sliced carrots and celery then cook a further 30
minutes.

Finally, add the potatoes which have been peeled and
cut into medium-sized cubes. Cook for another 30
minutes.

To Serve

Serve as is, or with pancakes or dumplings.
Invite people to splash Henderson's Relish on, to their
taste, and experience how it enhances the real
Yorkshire flavour of 'Ye Olde Yorkshire Hash'.

73

I submit this recipe in homage to Butler's Eatery, Brookhill, Sheffield, not a stone's throw from Leavygreave, home of Henderson's Relish. Butler's is, sadly, now gone but may Henderson's live for ever. Each day Butler's made huge Meat and Potato Pies which used to sit in the window, steaming hot and permeating marvellous aromas all around Leavygreave, and drawing all walks of Sheffield life into this fine Eatery. The recipe was secret but I feel sure my version is pretty near.

Baldwin's Meat & Potato Pie

To Serve 8
Ingredients

Filling
- 1½ lbs (750g) stewing beef
- 1½ lbs (750g) peeled potatoes cut into 1" cubes
- 2 large onions, finely chopped
- 2 dessertspoons fresh chopped parsley
- Salt & pepper
- 2 dessertspoons plain flour

- 2 tablespoons Henderson's Relish
- 1oz dripping

Rough Pastry
- ½ lb (250g) self-raising flour
- ½ lb (250g) plain flour
- Pinch of salt
- ½ lb (250g) home made beef dripping or lard
- Water as required

Method

Filling
Season the plain flour and place beef and flour in a polythene bag, shake to coat the beef (saves a mess).

Melt 1oz of dripping in a heavy saucepan, then fry off the onions, beef and parsley and add 6 generous shakes of Henderson's Relish.

When it is all going slightly brown add 2 pints (1.1 litres) of boiling water, stirring gently. Simmer for 1 hour and then add potatoes. Bring back to the boil and simmer until the potatoes are cooked, add 3 shakes of Henderson's Relish.

Remove from the heat and spoon the mixture into a suitable pie dish with just a little of the liquid. Keep the excess gravy hot for serving.

Pastry
Mix all the ingredients well, add water as required. Roll out the pastry to ½" (1cm) thick and cover the pie dish. Bake in a medium-hot oven for 30 minutes or so.

To Serve
Serve with Mushy Peas, Henderson's Relish and Gravy.

Cobblers
(Minced Beef with Dumplings)

To Serve 4
Ingredients

1¹/₂ lbs (750g) lean minced beef
2 medium onions
1oz (25g) beef dripping
1 tablespoon plain flour
¹/₄ pint (150ml) beef stock

2 tablespoons Henderson's Relish
Salt & pepper
4oz (100g) self-raising flour
2oz (50g) shredded suet

Method

Melt the dripping in a large frying pan and gently fry the onions until softened. Stir in the flour and continue to cook for 2 minutes stirring all the time. Gradually add the stock, stir until boiling then reduce the heat and simmer until the sauce thickens. Add the Henderson's Relish and the minced beef and season well. Turn into an oven-proof dish with a lid and cook in the centre of the oven at 180°C (gas 4) for 30 minutes.

Whilst the meat is cooking, prepare the dumplings. Mix together the flour and suet with sufficient water to make a firm but soft dough. Divide the dough into 8 portions and roll into balls—flour your hands before doing this. Place the dumplings on top of the mince, replace the lid and return to the oven for 20 minutes.

Turn the oven up to 200°C (gas 6) uncover the dish and cook for a further 10 minutes, or until the dumplings are crisp and golden.

To Serve

Serve with creamed potatoes, carrots and buttered cabbage—and pass the Henderson's.

Monday Rissoles

To Serve 2
Ingredients

8oz (250g) cold meat from the weekend joint (lamb or beef)
1 slice of white bread
2 onions
1 egg
1 tablespoon of Henderson's Relish
2 heaped tablespoons of flour
1oz (25g) dripping
Salt & pepper
Left over gravy from the joint

Method

Mince 1 of the onions, then the meat, then the bread. Mix these together in a large bowl and add salt and pepper to taste. Beat the egg together with the Henderson's, add to the mixture and stir in.

Divide the mixture into 4 and with floured hands form into cakes about $1/2$ inch (1cm) thick, then coat with seasoned flour.

Slice the other onion and fry gently in butter or oil in a small pan until soft, add the cold gravy and heat thoroughly until boiling.

Meanwhile heat the dripping in a frying pan and, when hot, fry the rissoles for about 5 minutes each side until golden brown.

To Serve

Serve the rissoles with chips, sliced green beans and the onion gravy.

VEGETARIAN DISHES

Hallamshire Hot Pot

To Serve 4–6
Ingredients

1lb (500g) large potatoes
1 head broccoli
3 sticks celery
2 leeks
1 small onion
8oz (250g) tomatoes
1 large can baked beans
1 small can red kidney beans

$1/2$ red pepper, chopped
$1/2$ yellow pepper, chopped
1 can (330ml) vegetable juice
3 tablespoons Henderson's Relish
2oz (50g) grated cheese
2 tablespoons olive oil
Salt & black pepper

Method

Peel and slice the potatoes into $1/4$ inch (.5cm) slices then par-boil in salted water. Just as they start to soften, remove from the heat and drain.

Prepare the vegetables: divide the broccoli into florets, slice the celery and leeks, chop the onion. Peel and chop the tomatoes and cut the peppers into slivers.

Grease a large oven-proof casserole dish and heat oven to 200°C (gas 6). Heat oil in a large frying pan and soften the onions, add all the other raw vegetables, except the tomatoes, and fry briskly stirring all the time, cook for about 5 minutes. Add the chopped tomatoes, baked beans, kidney beans, vegetable juice and the Henderson's Relish. Season well, bring to the boil then remove from the heat.

Line the bottom of the greased dish with half the potatoes then pour in the vegetable mix. Cover the mixture with the remaining potatoes and dot with butter. Cook, covered, in the oven for 20–30 minutes. Remove the lid and sprinkle with grated cheese, return the dish to the oven until the cheese has melted and the top is golden.

To Serve

Serve with hot crusty bread (or garlic bread if you prefer).

Mushroom Broth with Cheesy Croutons

To Serve 4
Ingredients

1¹/₂ lbs (750g) mushrooms
1 leek
1 celery stalk
1 tablespoon basmati rice
1¹/₂ pints (800ml) fresh vegetable stock
or
1 vegetable stock cube and 1¹/₂ pints water
2 tablespoons Henderson's Relish

1 glass red wine
Fresh parsley
2oz (50g) butter or 2 tablespoons virgin
   olive oil
2 French sticks
Cheddar cheese
Fresh chives
Salt and black & red pepper

Method

Broth
Chop the leek and celery then fry gently in the butter, or olive oil, whilst you chop the mushrooms. Add the mushrooms to the pan and continue to cook allowing the mushrooms to make their own liquid. Add the stock and 2 tablespoons of Henderson's Relish. Add the rice and season to taste. Pour in the red wine and simmer gently for 30–45 minutes.

Croutons
Cut 4 ¹/₂ inch (1cm) slices from a French stick. Toast these lightly, then butter (use garlic butter if preferred) and sprinkle with grated cheese and chives.

To Serve

Just before serving, pop the prepared croutons under a hot grill to melt the cheese. Ladle the soup into large bowls, float a crouton in each and sprinkle liberally with chopped parsley. Serve with the remainder of the French bread—you may prefer to make garlic bread as an accompaniment.

Tessa's Auntie Jessie's Savoury Rice

To Serve 2
Ingredients

6oz (150g) long grain rice
³/₄ pint (450ml) vegetable stock
¹/₄ pint (150ml) Henderson's Relish
1 bay leaf
2 tablespoons vegetable oil
1 large onion, thinly sliced or chopped
1 carrot, thinly sliced
1 pepper, thinly sliced
1 head of broccoli, separated into small florets
2 courgettes, thinly sliced
¹/₂ teaspoon dried basil (or ten fresh leaves)

4oz (125g) mushrooms, sliced or chopped
4oz (125g) parsnips, peeled and cubed
4oz (125g) grated Edam (or a vegetarian alternative)
4oz (125g) grated Mozzarella
2 large tomatoes, thinly sliced
1oz (25g) almonds, walnuts or roasted peanuts
1oz (25g) sultanas
Salt & black pepper
Parsley to garnish

Method

Rinse the rice well under cold running water. Turn into a bowl, cover with cold water and soak for 30 minutes. Drain, then put into a pan with the stock, Henderson's Relish and a bay leaf. Bring to the boil, cover the pan and simmer over a gentle heat for 30 minutes or until the rice is tender and the liquid absorbed. Remove the bay leaf after cooking.

Put the carrot, broccoli and parsnips into boiling salted water and simmer for 10–15 minutes until they are cooked but not soft, drain and keep warm.

Fifteen minutes before the rice is cooked, heat the oil in a large frying pan. Gently fry the onion, courgettes, mushrooms and pepper until they are soft but not brown. Add the remaining vegetables to the pan and fry briskly until they begin to caramelise.

Remove from the heat, stir in the basil, half the cheese and the rice and season to taste. Turn gently with a fork until heated through.

Spoon the mixture into a flameproof dish and arrange the tomato slices on top. Sprinkle with the remaining cheese and drizzle generously with Henderson's Relish then place under a hot grill for 3–4 minutes until the cheese is golden brown and bubbling.

To Serve

Sprinkle with chopped parsley and serve with a mixed salad.